This book is dedicated to those who are wise enough to dream and those who are brave enough to make their dreams come true.

Prolance

www.prolancewriting.com
California, USA
©2021 Lama Blaique

ISBN: 978-1-7371558-4-3

Table of Contents

"Dad!" exclaims Adam as he ran into the house. "This week at school we are talking about what we want to be when we grow up. Today, a doctor visited our class and told us about his job. He brought a stethoscope and was wearing a full white gown. I can't wait for tomorrow, it will be even more exciting. The teacher promised us that a famous basketball player will come! Can you believe it, I wonder who it might be?! Every day a different person will visit us. I think on Wednesday an engineer will come and on Thursday a librarian. I forgot who will be coming to visit us on Friday.

The teacher told all of us in class that we should start thinking about what we want to be when we grow up."

"You can be whoever you want to be," Dad tells him. "However it might be too early to decide now, you might change your mind later. The important thing is to be a good Muslim."

"In what way, Dad?" Adam asks.

"Well Adam, a good Muslim is someone who is kind, caring and helps others. He is someone who has strong will power and good knowledge. These things make him shine like a star," Dad explains.

"I love stars, without them the sky is dark and boring. Mmm, can I be a scientist and still be a good Muslim? I want to be the best scientist in the world and find a cure for cancer. But I have not heard of any Muslims who have done something important. You know Dad, like Bill Gates or Einstein."

"How about I tell you a story every day about a historical famous Muslim who did something important that helped the world become a better place?"

"Yes! I am so excited.

"Great. Let's go back in time and meet each one of them?" Dad says. "First we will meet Abbas Ibn Firnas."

"Abbas who?" Asks Adam.

"Haha, Ibn Firnas, I bet you've never heard of him, I am sure a lot of people haven't either. Are you ready? Step into my time machine and we will go back one thousand two hundred years!"

1

Abbas Ibn Firnas
The Father of Aviation

"Abbas Ibn Firnas was a curious inventor who lived in Andalusia. Andalusia was a great Muslim kingdom ruled by a just ruler. The people of Andalusia loved to learn new things all the time. Ibn Firnas was a scholar who loved poetry, physics, philosophy and astrology. He invented the pen when the use of a quill, a pen made from a bird's feather dipped in ink, was common. He also invented many ways for making transparent glass from sand. But he was mostly famous for his attempts to fly.

He spent years studying and researching elements of flying such as the impact of air, body weight and air resistance. Then, he eventually succeeded in creating a basic flying machine." Dad says as they approached a big crowd.

"On this sunny day, Adam, in the year 875 A.D. in Cordoba, the city where Abbas lived, people gathered to witness what would be the first successful attempt of flying in the history of humanity."

Adam and his dad stood among the crowd anxiously waiting for Abbas to make his move. Abbas flew out and was able to use his machine to fly over Cordoba for a few minutes.

Suddenly Adam hears Dad calling him.

"Adam! Watch out!" Abbas Ibn Firnas was about to crash into them!

"While his attempt to fly was successful and paved the way for other scientists to further develop the aviation mechanism, the same couldn't be said about Abbas' landing techniques that day. Thank God Abbas survived with minor injuries to his back as his flying model hit the ground. Abbas was not discouraged and continued in his aviation experiments. He later improved the quality of the wings and included a tail for smoother landings just like birds have for alighting," Dad explains as they head back home.

"Dad!" Adam shouts as he steps out of the car and starts hovering all around the garage with his arms stretched out like an airplane, "Ibn Firnas is such a brave guy!"

"You're right Adam, if it weren't for people like Abbas who was curious and brave, we would not have been able to travel across continents in a short time and enjoy a better life," Dad adds. "You see Adam, this is what I call a true star, he brightens the way for others to have a better life."

Yacub Al-Ansari (Abu Yusuf)
The Grand Judge

"Dad I told my friends at school today all about Abbas! You should've seen Samir, he was jumping up and down with excitement as I was telling them how brave Abbas was.

"Well, this is great Adam, wait until you hear today's story then," his father says.

Adam and his dad hop into their time machine, as if it was becoming part of their daily routine. Adam puts on the seatbelt, excited for a new adventure through time.

Adam presses the car engine button eagerly. Within a few minutes, they find themselves sitting in a very fancy and huge castle. There is a huge feast set in front of them for hundreds of people.

"Yacub Al-Ansari was also known as Abu Yusuf. He was born in Baghdad, Iraq in the year 798 A.D. At the age of 10, his father passed away and he grew up as an orphan living in a poor house with his mom. Despite his love for learning and reading, his mom wanted him to work so he can help her financially. She found him a job at a tailor shop. Next to the tailor's shop was a masjid where Abu Hanifa, a very famous Islamic scholar at the time, gave lectures. Abu Yusuf would sneak out of the tailor's shop and spend hours attending Abu Hanifa's classes. He enjoyed learning about Islam and its teachings. Abu Hanifa started noticing the boy and knew that he had talent and would grow up to achieve something, so he gave him special attention.

However, the tailor notified his mom that Abu Yusuf was disappearing during the day. Each time the mom would look for him and bring him back from the masjid to the shop. Until one time she became really mad from all of this. She marched into the masjid, interrupted the lecture, took her son, and walked straight to Abu Hanifa. In a harsh tone, she addressed the scholar saying, 'No one spoiled this boy but you! We need money to live but instead of working, my son is running away to listen to your lectures. This is all because of you!'

Abu Hanifa's reply was very strange, he politely said, 'You silly woman, I am teaching him how to eat Falooda with pistachio butter.'

Falooda was a very rare and expensive kind of dessert that was eaten only by kings and sultans at that time.

Abu Yusuf grew up to become a very famous Islamic scholar and the successor of Abu Hanifa in the Hanafi prejudice. He was also appointed as the Grand Judge (Qadi) by the Khalifa (the Muslim ruler). It was the first time in Islamic history that someone receives such a title.

We are now attending the banquette set by the Khalifa (the Muslim ruler) where Abu Yusuf is invited. Can you see him? He is sitting to the right of the Khalifa."

Adam shifts his head forward to have a clearer view. Abu Yusuf is being offered a dessert that he has never seen in his life before. The Khalifa tells him, "This is Falooda, you should try it Abu Yusuf, it is something we only serve on special occasions."

As Abu Yusuf tries the fancy desert, he has a huge smile on his face. Apparently, he remembered his teacher's words back then. Indeed, Allah never fails those who believe in him!

8

3

Salahuddin Ayubi
The Warrior King

Adam and his dad find themselves sitting in an old dusty tent with noises of people and horses moving back and forth. Adam peaks his head out of the tent to try to see what is going on as his dad starts telling him the story of the warrior king.

"Yusuf Bin Ayub was born in the year 1138 A.D. in Iraq to a Kurdish military family. He was also known as Salahuddin, which means righteousness of faith in Arabic, and Al Malik Al-Nasir, the Warrior King. Both his parents had the same vision about him even before they met each other. They both wished to have a young boy who would grow up to free Al-Aqsa mosque from the Crusaders' invasion. His tough military upbringing by his father made him a brave, persistent and shrewd fighter. He fought for many years to expand and strengthen the Muslim countries.

He had one big dream: to free Al-Aqsa mosque. Why Al-Aqsa mosque? Because it is the third holy place for Muslims after Makkah and Madinah. It is a dear place to the heart of our Prophet Muhammad (saw) and the place where Prophet Issa was born as well.

One of his famous quotes was, 'I'd be ashamed to laugh while the Al-Aqsa is in captivity.'

On July 4, 1187 A.D the battle of Hittin took place between the Crusader state that had 63 thousand warriors and Salahuddin's army that had only around 12 thousand soldiers. This famous battle, that was planned and led by Salahuddin, changed the face of history. The Muslims, despite their small army, won the battle and were able to free Jerusalem from Crusade occupation.

Here we are Adam, one week later, and after 88 years of occupation, the yellow flags of the Warrior King hovering above Al-Aqsa mosque," his dad explains.

Both Adam and his dad step out of the tent and start to march with the crowds as they chant in celebration of their victory. Adam could not take his eyes off the leader's shiny armour. Could that be Salahuddine, he thinks.

As they return back home his dad explains to him that the major victories that Salahuddin won did not make him arrogant. On the contrary, they made him more compassionate and more humble which earned him more respect. At one point, one of his fiercest enemies, Richard the Lion Heart, became extremely sick. When Salahuddin found out, he sent Richard his personal doctor.

Salahuddin spent the majority of his life fighting, and all of his money went to the protection of Muslim countries. When he passed away in 1193 A.D., at the age of 56, his family didn't have enough money to arrange his funeral.

4

Mimar Sinan
A Passionate Architect

"Now Adam today is day four of our adventure and I am going to share with you the story of a person who I hold dear respect for." Adam's dad says.

"Who is he dad? Say come on, say!" Adam shouts excitedly.

"Ok, how about I take you to see his achievements. His work is the reason I decided to become an architect myself"

"Oh wow ! So he made buildings too?"

"Yes, huge ones." His dad explains as they go inside the time machine and close the doors behind them.

They step out into a dusty construction site with workers all around as busy as bees in a beehive.

"Mimar Sinan, meaning architect Sinan, was born in Istanbul, Turkey in 1490. He was one of the most influential Islamic architects in history. So how did he get this title? Sinan first started learning about architecture and sculpture by helping his dad in his workshop where he worked as a stone mason.

When he reached the age of 24, Sinan joined the Ottoman army where he took on many ranks. He worked on different building projects during his 26 years of service. Later, he became the Chief of Imperial Architects. Sinan wanted to build something different, he wanted to offer his country something new! He had a dream of building a masjid with the biggest dome in the world! While many people at that time thought that was impossible, he was able to build the Selimiye masjid with the largest dome, in addition to 4 minarets each at 83 meters high!"

"How tall is that dad?"

"It is equal to around a 25-story building!"

"But dad how is that even possible!" Adam is interrupted as a fleet of construction men pass by them. They are moving one of the minarets on a big carriage. Leading them is a tall and strongly built man. He is too busy giving instructions to the workers in one hand and holding what seems to be like a drawing of a masjid in the other.

"Sinan also designed the Suleymaniye mosque, which is considered to our present time a significant Islamic monument," Adam's dad continues. "It took him seven years to finish this huge project since it contained a mosque, a kitchen, a hospital and a school. So, it is no surprise that the Suleymaniye masjid is Istanbul's second largest mosque.

The great Mimar Sinan died in Istanbul in 1588 A.D. at the age of 98. Inspired by his Islamic faith and passion for architecture, he was able to design and work on more than 374 buildings and structures."

5 Abu Al-Kasim Al-Shabbi
The Young Poet

"Are you ready for today's adventure Adam?" Dad asks.

"Yes, I am dad, but I need some time because I am writing a goodbye card for my class teacher. She is leaving the country in two weeks. I am kind of sad, I am going to miss her. She is the best."

"Well then, I think the adventure we are going on today might give you some ideas on what to write in your card."

"OK, let's start then" exclaims Adam.

"It is not the number of years that you spend on this earth that matters, but rather what you achieve during those years. This is exactly what can be said about the Tunisian poet Abu Al-Kasim Al-Shabbi who was born in Tozeur in 1909."

"Is this where he lived?" Adam asks as he and his father step inside a huge old building.

"No, this is the public library where his work is still kept. At the age of 22, Abu Al-Kasim Al-Shabbi was diagnosed with a severe heart problem that limited his daily life activities. He wrote in his diaries that he was incredibly sad when the doctor told him about his condition. He felt lonely and isolated because he was no longer able to join his friends in any outdoor activities. He spent most of his days resting. Sometimes the path that Allah chooses for us might look difficult at first, yet a lot of good is always hidden beneath the bad.

Abu Al-Kasim's medical condition gave him a lot of spare time to focus on what he loves, which was reading and studying Arabic and European literature and poetry. This helped him get in touch with his own feelings and ideas and produce what would later be considered the best poems in the modern Arabic era.

In his writings, he challenged the status quo and discussed matters that people of his time where dealing with. After his father passed away, Abu Al-Kasim felt very sad. He loved his father and had a special relationship with him. Grieving over his father made his heart even weaker, and, after years of illness, he passed away at the very early age of 25. However, he left more than 75 beautiful poems that inspired the youth to be positive, persistent and optimistic."

"What is this letter?" Adam asks curiously as he unfolds it and starts reading one of Abu Al-Kasem's poems out loud:

O rise up and march on the paths of Life -- Those who sleep will be left behind -- You were born free as a breeze As a light in a dusky sky -- Like a chanting bird wherever you go -- Singing songs inspired by the Divine -- Roaming gaily amidst roses of morn -- Basking in light wherever you find

"Abu Al-Kasim, indeed did accomplish in around 5 years what would take others a lifetime to achieve. Your teacher, Adam, might be leaving the school and I know this makes you sad. But you have to think about the possibilities. You may get a new teacher who is as nice as she was. You never know. I want you to look back at the time you spent together in the class and think about all the interesting things that you learned from her. It would be nice to thank her for all that right? Remember what might appear to be bad may be holding good surprises for us in the end."

6 Muhammad Mitwali Shaarawi
Preacher of the Century

"Now that Ramadan is approaching, I thought it would be useful to go on this next adventure. You know Adam how important charity is, especially in Ramadan. But have you ever thought about doing an ever-lasting charity?"

"Ever-lasting! How is that possible?" Adam exclaims.

"Let us go back in time around one hundred years or so to meet our new star. Muhammad was born in a humble family in the village of Daqadus, Egypt on April 5, 1911. Both his parents were dedicated farmers, and perhaps this is why he also dreamt of spending his life to working in the land. However, he had an exceptional talent in Arabic and Quranic studies. He was able to memorize the entire Quran by the age of 11."

Adam and his father find themselves standing in a very small, humble room filled with books. "What are all these books dad?" Adam asks as he is about to trip over one of them.

"Muhammad's father saw how bright his son was and wanted him to continue his education in the capital city of Cairo at one of the most prestigious Islamic universities at the time, Al-Azhar. However, the 26-year-old young man was smart and decided to pull a trick on his father so he would let him stay in the village. He started asking him for dozens and dozens of books about Arabic language, Quran, history and heritage thinking this would make his dad change his mind. His father, patiently and thoughtfully bought him all the books," Adam's dad replies.

Adam starts to laugh and says, "What a smart boy Muhammad was!"

"But eventually his dad convinced him to go and he began his life chànging journey at Al-Azhar University where he grew fond of the various Islamic subjects he learned there. After graduating, he took on different teaching posts in prominent universities in Egypt, Saudi Arabia and Algeria. At some point in his life, he became the Minister of Endowments in Egypt. He was in charge of Islamic affairs for Muslims in Egypt and other Muslim countries.

He shared his wide knowledge on Quranic studies for the first time when he was hosted on a TV show. He became a worldwide sensation in the Islamic world and was regarded as the "Preacher of the Century." His exceptional talent laid in his ability to simplify difficult verses of the Quran for the audience. He won the hearts of thousands of people who would listen to his lectures for hours. They could sense the love and passion about Islam as he talked.

Although Shaarawi died at the age of 87 in 1998, people still enjoy reading his books, watching his TV programs and listening to his lectures. One would wonder, how do people still remember him decades after his death? The answer is simple. Muhammad put his heart into explaining the Quran, and did so with full dedication and love. He wanted people to benefit from his knowledge and the result was an ever-lasting charity for him."

"What do you mean dad, put his heart into explaining the Quran?"

"I mean he did it with love Adam," Dad explains

Safiyu-Rahman Mubarakpuri
The Sealed Nectar

"Now Adam I know how much you love books so I decided that in this next adventure we meet an author who wrote a very special book, what do you say?"

"Ok Dad, I am all ears let's go," Adam says as he pushes away his computer to the corner of his bed and heads towards the car time machine with his father.

"Safiyu-Rahman was an Islamic scholar, author and most importantly a passionate lover of Sirah, the biography of Prophet Muhammad (saw). He grew up in India where he learned Quran, Arabic language and other Islamic studies. As a young man, he received the Alim (Scholar) Certification and began teaching at several Islamic schools.

Safiyu-Rahman had a golden opportunity to share his love and knowledge about the Prophet Muhammad when the Muslim World League in 1976 launched a worldwide competition for writing the Prophet's biography. During the several months following the advertisement, Safiyu-Rahman was focused on nothing but writing a book about the life of the Prophet. He put a lot of effort into this book, nothing was dearer to him than Muhammad (saw). He, along with 171 participants, submitted his book to the committee."

"What is all this noise?" Adam asks his dad as they find themselves sitting in a huge stadium with hundreds of people cheering all around them.

"It is the day when they will be announcing the winner of the best book Adam," his dad shouts across the crowd.

As the committee enters the stadium, the noise of the crowd starts to disappear. Adam is so excited that he could hear his own heartbeat. The time has come to announce the winner! The book by Safiyu-Rahman wins first prize! The crowd starts clapping and cheering and so does Adam with a huge smile on his face!

When they return home, his dad continues the story. "The book was titled The Sealed Nectar and was published in three languages, Arabic, English and Urdu because of how popular it became. It is still considered a main reference for anyone who wishes to know more about the life of our dear Prophet. With Allah's help, love and hard work, Safiyu-Rahman gave the Muslim world a precious gift, scented with prophetic love."

8

Abdul-Rahman Al-Sumait
Rejuvenating Africa

"Remember Adam when we first started this adventure you wanted to find out more about Muslims who did something important? This person I am going to tell you about today helped a whole continent," his dad says.

"What?! A whole continent. Amazing!"

"Put on your cap and grab a bottle of water before you go into the time machine."

"Why dad?" Adam exclaims impatiently.

"Because it is hot in Africa!" explains his dad.

Adam and his dad stand in the shade of a small tree facing a volunteer camp. His dad continues by saying, "Abdul-Rahman was a Kuwaiti doctor who went on a hearty mission to bring Africa back to life. He extensively helped millions of people find Islamic faith and live a better life by building camps like this. He visited more than 29 African countries such as Kenya, Malawi and Tanzania.

As Abdul Rahman was standing in front of a volunteer camp in Africa one day, a young lady's scream grabbed his attention. The woman had a sick baby in her arms. The doctors at the camp refused to offer the baby any medical help, explaining there was no hope for him to live. They would rather give the medication to other babies who still had a chance. Dr. Abdul-Rahman approached the young woman and asked her how much money she would need to take care of her baby. He was surprised when she told him the amount, it was equal to the price of a soda can! He felt sorry for her and decided to help her out for as long as the baby needed.

Twelve years later, an African lady went to see him with her young boy while he was working in one of the camps. She explained that her son wanted to volunteer with Dr. Abdul-Rahman and help other Muslims. The young boy had a beautiful face, he had memorized the Quran and knows both Arabic and African languages. Dr. Abdul-Rahman did not recognize the woman at first.

The mother said, "This is the baby who you saved 12 years ago when other doctors refused to help! Dr. Abdul-Rahman could not believe what he heard! He was overwhelmed with joy. He went down on his knees and thanked Allah. How gracious is Allah. For the price of one soda can, that baby's life was saved. Who knew that this young Muslim man would end up helping other needy people years later?

Dr. Abdul-Rahaman passed away in 2013 and his life carried one message: Do good to humanity because Allah is gracious, and Jannah (Heaven) is beautiful."

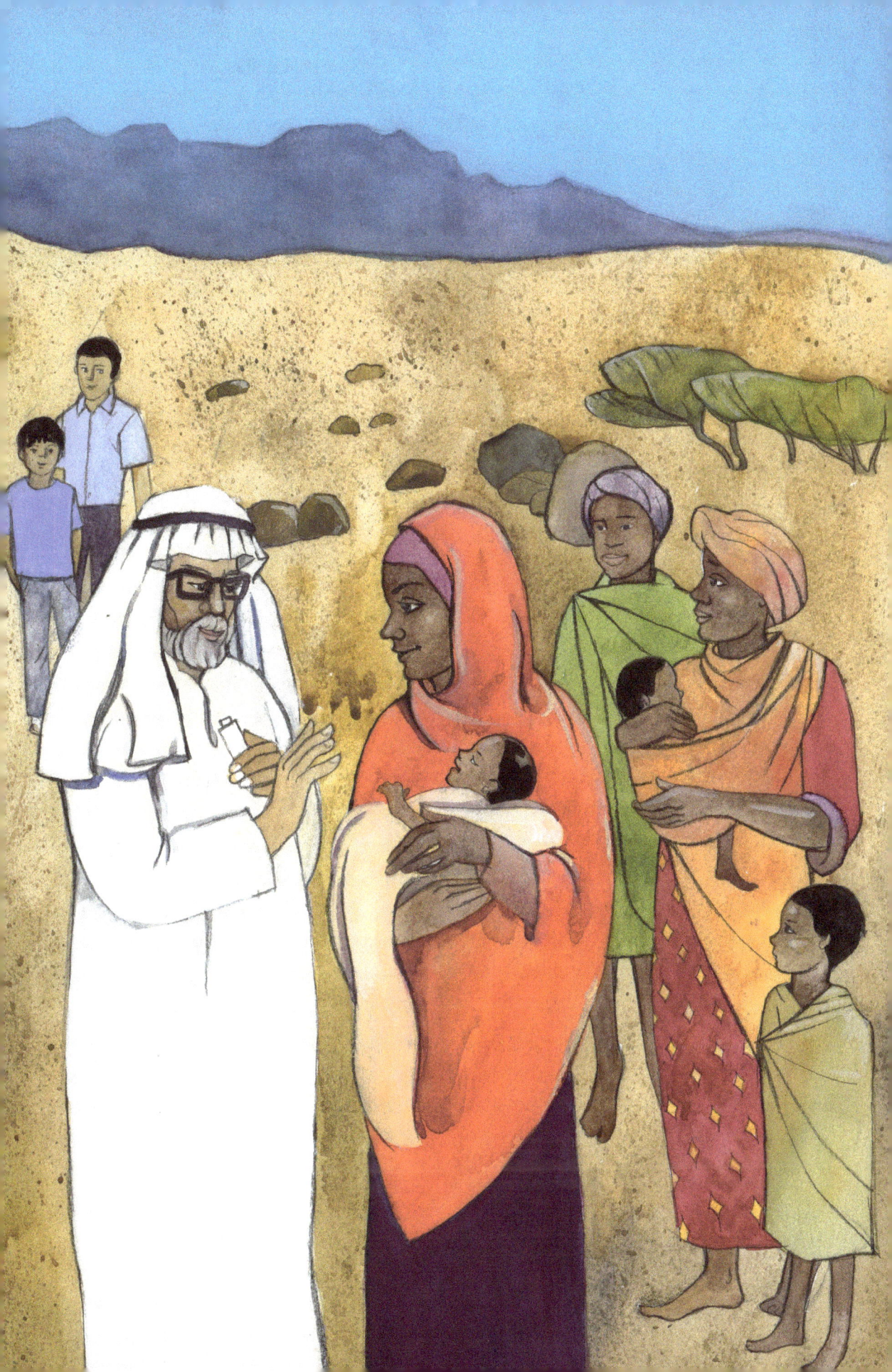

9   Abu Aynayn Al-Shuayshea
The Lark of the Nile

"How was the Quran lesson today?" Adam's dad asks him.

"It was very good, but the Tajweed classes are a bit hard. Why do we have to learn reading Quran this way, why can't we just read it like we read a storybook?!" Adam exclaims.

"Angel Jibril taught Prophet Muhammad (saw) how to recite Quran using Tajweed. This is the correct way to read Quran. It helps us focus on the letters and meanings of the words. Actually, today's adventure will be about a person who loved reciting Quran," Adams dad explains.

"Ok, let's go Dad!" Adam shouts.

"It is 1922 and Abu Aynayn was the 12th child of a poor family in the city of Bila, Egypt. His dad passed away when he was only 9 years old. His mom grew worried because she did not know how she will be able to take care of 12 children on her own. Little did she know that Abu Aynayn would be the main provider for the whole family years later."

Adam and his dad find themselves sitting on the dusty ground at the back of a small room. The roof is topped with palm trees scattered all over it with arbitrary rays of light sneaking in.

"This is Abu Aynayn's school, Adam. It is his turn to recite Quran now, listen carefully."

Both Adam and his dad are enchanted by Aby Aynayn's beautiful voice and Quran recitation. When he finishes reciting, Adam's dad continues, "His beautiful voice and Quran recitation grabbed the attention of his teacher who advised his mom to take him to special Quran recitation classes. At the age of 14, he was invited to recite Quran at an Islamic event. When he entered the hall, he was shocked to see the huge crowd. He felt very intimidated, especially because there were young boys his age among the audience. At first, they did not take him seriously at all and started giggling, laughing and making fun of his young age.

However, after he finished his recitation and stepped down from the stage, the audience gathered around him to congratulate him on his beautiful reading. He had tears in his eyes and could not believe it! Since then, he became one of the most famous Quran reciters of his times. He got a good job at one of the famous radio stations and was invited to many worldwide Islamic events.

In 1966, at the age of 44, he suffered from a serious sickness that affected his vocal cords. As a result, he was not able to recite Quran for a long period of time. He had a favourite supplication that he always recited: 'Oh Allah, don't deprive me from being a servant to your Holy Quran until I meet you.'

He believed that Allah will not let him down, and after some time his voice came back. His Quran recitations were recorded and are still played on radios till this day. He is remembered as the Lark of the Nile because of his beautiful recitation of the Holy Quran."

10 Muhammad Ali Clay
The Greatest Boxer

"Dad, I had a fight at school today with a boy who was always pulling Janet's hair." Adam says.

"And what did you do?"

"I punched him!"

"Oh, you did! You know violence does not solve everything Adam. You should have gone to the teacher and complained. But I am glad that you defended your friend Janet. Next time you either try to talk to him and convince him not to pull Janet's hair anymore or tell the teacher. I did not know you could punch, show me how you did it."

"Like that," Adam says while swinging his right hand in a strong manner.

"Well then, I think it will be a good idea to take you to a boxing arena for our last adventure. We will meet Muhammad Ali who was the greatest boxer of all time. But unlike what you may think, he did not solve everything with a punch," his dad said jokingly.

"Cassius Clay (Muhammad Ali) was born to a Baptist family in Kentucky, in the United States of America in 1942. When he was 12 years old, his bike got stolen. He was truly angry and told the police officer that he wanted to beat up the thief. The police officer was a boxing trainer and advised him that before he challenged anyone he should learn how to fight properly. That was the turning point in his life. After years of rigid training he became a boxing champion

In the early 1960s, he started attending Islamic lectures with some friends. There, he found out for the first time that Allah is one, Muhammad (saw) is his Prophet, and the Quran is Allah's words. The moment he heard this, he knew in his heart that this was what he was searching for all his life. He bravely became a Muslim and changed him name to Muhammad Ali. Muhammad means worthy of all praises and Ali means the most high.

After winning the world boxing championship for the first time, he was asked by one reporter if this is the happiest moment in his life. He said, "No! The happiest moment in my life was when I became a Muslim."

As Adam and his dad reach the arena, they are caught up by the cheering crowd. They can hardly reach their places. "Is that him fighting in the arena?" Adam asks his dad.

"Yes!"

He was famous for his charming and charismatic character. He had amazingly fast feet and swift fists. He describes himself in the wrestling arena saying: *I float like a butterfly and sting like a bee.* He was called the greatest boxer of all time because he won 56 times and lost only 5.

In a TV interview, Muhammad Ali was once asked if he had a bodyguard. He did not need one, no one needs a bodyguard. Muhammad Ali explains why by saying, "No, I have only one bodyguard, he has no eyes - though he sees, he has no ears - though he hears. He remembers everything without the aid of mind and memory. When He wishes to create a thing, He just orders it to be and it comes into existence. But His order does not convey the words which take the tongue to form or the sound that is carried by the ears. He hears the secrets of our quite thoughts. Who's that? That's God, Allah. He's my bodyguard. He is your bodyguard. He's the Supreme, the Wise."

In 1989, Muhammad Ali was diagnosed with Parkinson's disease. Although this disease did not affect his mental capacity, it became difficult for him to speak or to even move. The greatest boxer of all time was not saddened by this, however. He considered the disease as a test from Allah. He faced this test with faith and courage. He passed away in 2016 after spending years helping Muslim communities and donating a large portion of his wealth to charity.

Adam's father tucked him into bed after they returned from their last adventure. It is getting late and they were both tired.

"Now Adam we went back in time and met 10 amazing Muslim heroes who worked hard to reach their goals. Their accomplishments are of great value to humanity. Whether an architect, a poet, an athlete or a warrior, each did something good for others. I hope their lives inspire you and help you to decide what you want to become when you grow up."

"Now I know dad that I have not one, but many options to choose from. Thank you Dad," Adam says as sleep takes over him.

The Author

Lama Blaique was born in Beirut, Lebanon. As a dedicated Muslim mother of two young boys, she became interested in children's literature and the representation of Muslim figures through storytelling. Lama has been living in Dubai, United Arab Emirates for more than 10 years now. She is an assistant professor of business management and when she is not teaching and conducting research, she loves to read, travel, and explore.
Instagram @blaique_lama

The Illustrator

Jenny Reynish is an artist and illustrator working mainly in children's publishing and has created a wide variety of illustrations for US and UK publishers. Her individual and decorative style was sparked by a Persian rug from Isfahan, inherited from her aunt. She loves the colors and decorative patterns of the Middle East and India, and finds much inspiration from living by the sea. She works in watercolor, oil, and linoprint.
www.magiccarpetpics.co.uk

www.ingramcontent.com/pod-product-compliance
Lightning Source LLC
Chambersburg PA
CBHW060803150426
42813CB00059B/2868